Think Positive, Stay Positive

summersdale

THINK POSITIVE, STAY POSITIVE

An Hachette UK Company
www.hachette.co.uk

Summersdale Publishers Ltd
Part of Octopus Publishing Group Limited
Carmelite House
50 Victoria Embankment
LONDON
EC4Y 0DZ
UK

www.summersdale.com

Printed and bound in Malta

ISBN: 978-1-78685-035-5

To...

From...

When life looks like it's falling apart, it may just be falling in place.

Beverly Solomon

IT AIN'T NO USE
PUTTING UP YOUR
UMBRELLA TILL
IT RAINS.

Alice Hegan Rice

DON'T WORRY ABOUT
IT. THE RIGHT THING WILL
COME AT THE **RIGHT TIME.**

Danielle Steel

Start and end each day with a positive thought.

HAPPINESS CONSISTS NOT IN HAVING MUCH, BUT IN BEING CONTENT WITH LITTLE.

Marguerite Gardiner

Say and do something positive that will help the situation; it doesn't take any brains to complain.

Robert A. Cook

IF YOU HAVE GOOD
THOUGHTS THEY WILL SHINE
OUT OF YOUR FACE LIKE
SUNBEAMS AND YOU WILL
ALWAYS **LOOK LOVELY**.

Roald Dahl

It's always too early to quit.

Norman Vincent Peale

STAY SUNNY ON
THE OUTSIDE
AND WARM ON
THE INSIDE.

POSITIVE ANYTHING IS BETTER THAN NEGATIVE NOTHING.

Elbert Hubbard

Do a little more each day than you think you possibly can.

Lowell Thomas

WORK ON WHAT IS REAL
RATHER THAN WORRY
ABOUT WHAT IS UNREAL.

Elizabeth George

NEVER LOOK
BACKWARDS OR
YOU'LL FALL DOWN
THE STAIRS.

Rudyard Kipling

POSITIVE
ACTIONS LEAD
TO POSITIVE
RESULTS.

WORRY IS AS USELESS
AS A HANDLE ON
A **SNOWBALL**.

Mitzi Chandler

Once you replace negative thoughts with positive ones, you'll start having positive results.

Willy Nelson

LOOK ON EVERY
EXIT AS BEING
AN ENTRANCE
SOMEWHERE ELSE.

Tom Stoppard

Keep
hope
in your
heart.

What makes the desert beautiful... Is that somewhere it hides a well.

Antoine de Saint-Exupéry

YOU ARE NEVER TOO OLD
TO SET ANOTHER GOAL OR
TO DREAM A NEW DREAM.

C. S. Lewis

POSITIVITY IS
THE SECRET.

ENTHUSIASM MOVES THE WORLD.

Arthur Balfour

EVERY MOMENT HAS ITS
PLEASURES AND **ITS HOPE.**

Jane Austen

I may not have gone
where I intended to go,
but I think I have ended
up where I needed to be.

Douglas Adams

THERE ARE TWO WAYS
OF SPREADING LIGHT: TO
BE THE CANDLE OR THE
MIRROR THAT REFLECTS IT.

Edith Wharton

SAY GOOD WORDS, THINK GOOD THINGS, DO GOOD DEEDS.

A happy life consists not in the absence, but in the mastery of hardships.

Helen Keller

SINCE THE HOUSE IS ON FIRE LET US WARM OURSELVES.

Italian proverb

THE SUN IS NEW EACH DAY.

Heraclitus

Whoever is happy will make others happy too.

Anne Frank

Inside every setback hides opportunity.

LET YOUR HOOK BE
ALWAYS CAST; IN
THE POOL WHERE
YOU LEAST EXPECT IT,
THERE WILL BE FISH.

Ovid

Yesterday is gone. Tomorrow has not yet come. We have only today. Let us begin.

Mother Teresa

IT IS OFTEN IN THE DARKEST
SKIES THAT WE SEE THE
BRIGHTEST STARS.

Richard Evans

DO NOT THINK OF
TODAY'S FAILURES,
BUT OF THE SUCCESS
THAT MAY COME
TOMORROW.

Helen Keller

ACT AS IF WHAT YOU
DO MAKES A DIFFERENCE.
IT DOES.

William James

POSITIVE
MIND,
POSITIVE
FEELINGS,
POSITIVE
LIFE.

The best is yet to do.

William Shakespeare

YOU'RE WORRIED ABOUT
WHAT-IFS. WELL, WHAT IF
YOU **STOPPED WORRYING?**

Shannon Celebi

DO SOMETHING TODAY THAT YOUR FUTURE SELF WILL THANK YOU FOR.

KEEPING BUSY AND
MAKING OPTIMISM
A WAY OF LIFE CAN
RESTORE YOUR FAITH
IN YOURSELF.

Lucille Ball

If things go wrong, don't go with them.

Roger Babson

REGARD MISTAKES AS TEACHERS, **NOT JUDGES!**

Tae Yun Kim

Do not anticipate trouble, or worry about what may never happen. Keep in the sunlight.

Benjamin Franklin

WORRY IS LIKE A
ROCKING-CHAIR.
IT GIVES YOU
SOMETHING TO
DO BUT GETS YOU
NOWHERE.

Wayne Bennett

Good things are going to happen!

If you don't like how things are, change it! You're not a tree.

Jim Rohn

THE MOST IMPORTANT
THING IS TO ENJOY YOUR
LIFE – TO BE HAPPY – IT'S
ALL THAT MATTERS.

Audrey Hepburn

In three words I can sum up everything I've learned about life: it goes on.

Robert Frost

LET REALITY BE
REALITY. LET THINGS
FLOW NATURALLY
FORWARD IN
WHATEVER WAY
THEY LIKE.

Lao Tzu

DON'T COUNT THE DAYS...

MAKE THE DAYS COUNT.

WHEN YOU HAVE
CONFIDENCE, YOU CAN
HAVE A LOT OF FUN.

Joe Namath

YOUR OPINION
IS VALUABLE.

The dreamers are the saviours of the world.

James Allen

ONLY THOSE WHO NEVER
STEP, **NEVER STUMBLE.**

Richard Paul Evans

BELIEVE YOU CAN
AND YOU'RE
HALFWAY THERE.

Theodore Roosevelt

What you do today can improve all your tomorrows.

Ralph Marston

Be positive, patient and persistent.

I HAVE FOUND
THAT IF YOU LOVE
LIFE, LIFE WILL LOVE
YOU BACK.

Arthur Rubinstein

ONE WHO CONTINUES
TO ADVANCE WILL WIN
IN THE END.

Daisaku Ikeda

HAVE
CONFIDENCE
IN YOUR OWN
ABILITY.

There is no wealth but life.

John Ruskin

NOTHING TO ME FEELS
AS GOOD AS LAUGHING
INCREDIBLY HARD.

Steve Carell

YOU NEVER LOSE
BY LOVING. YOU
ALWAYS LOSE BY
HOLDING BACK.

Barbara De Angelis

Opportunity comes to those who create it.

**Create the kind of self
that you will be happy to
live with all your life.**

Golda Meir

LIFE IS VERY
INTERESTING. IN THE END,
SOME OF YOUR GREATEST
PAINS BECOME YOUR
GREATEST STRENGTHS.

Drew Barrymore

TAKE TIME TO DO WHAT YOUR SOUL WANTS!

YOU MUST EXPECT
GREAT THINGS FROM
YOURSELF BEFORE YOU
CAN DO THEM.

Michael Jordan

TODAY, FILL YOUR
CUP OF LIFE WITH
SUNSHINE AND
LAUGHTER.

Dodinsky

CHALLENGES ARE OPPORTUNITIES TO GROW.

Most people have never learned that one of the main aims in life is to enjoy it.

Samuel Butler

THE BEST WAY TO
CHEER YOURSELF UP
IS TO TRY TO CHEER
SOMEBODY ELSE UP.

Mark Twain

Setbacks are the hurdles of life. Jump them!

Ride the energy of your own unique spirit.

Gabrielle Roth

LIFE IS A GREAT BIG
CANVAS, AND YOU
SHOULD THROW ALL THE
PAINT ON IT YOU CAN.

Danny Kaye

WHO CARES ABOUT WINNING OR LOSING? LIFE IS MORE FUN WHEN TAKING PART.

WHAT YOU PLANT NOW, YOU WILL HARVEST LATER.

Og Mandino

LIFE IS A HELLUVA LOT
MORE FUN IF YOU SAY
'YES' **RATHER THAN 'NO'.**

Richard Branson

Follow your own star.

Dante Alighieri

LEARN FROM
YESTERDAY, LIVE FOR
TODAY, HOPE FOR
TOMORROW. THE
IMPORTANT THING
IS NOT TO STOP
QUESTIONING.

Albert Einstein

MAKE A WISH... THEN MAKE IT COME TRUE!

**Because you are alive,
everything is possible.**

Nhat Hanh

TO LIVE IS THE RAREST
THING IN THE WORLD.
MOST PEOPLE EXIST,
THAT IS ALL.

Oscar Wilde

OPTIMISM IS A HAPPINESS
MAGNET. IF YOU STAY
POSITIVE, GOOD THINGS
AND GOOD PEOPLE WILL
BE DRAWN TO YOU.

Mary Lou Retton

Celebrate every victory and celebrate others' too!

WE DON'T STOP
PLAYING BECAUSE
WE GROW OLD;
WE GROW OLD
BECAUSE WE STOP
PLAYING.

George Bernard Shaw

In order to carry
a positive action we
must develop here a
positive vision.

Dalai Lama

EVERYTHING THAT IS
DONE IN THE WORLD IS
DONE BY HOPE.

Martin Luther

A head full of dreams has no space for fears.

Anonymous

ALL LIFE IS AN
EXPERIMENT. THE
MORE EXPERIMENTS
YOU MAKE THE
BETTER.

Ralph Waldo Emerson

BELIEVE IN MAGIC AND YOU WILL FIND IT.

No one can make you feel inferior without your consent.

Eleanor Roosevelt

FIRST SAY TO YOURSELF
WHAT YOU WOULD BE;
AND THEN DO WHAT YOU
HAVE TO DO.

Epictetus

MAY YOU LIVE
ALL THE DAYS OF
YOUR LIFE.

Jonathan Swift

FORGET PAST MISTAKES.
FORGET FAILURES. FORGET
EVERYTHING EXCEPT WHAT
YOU'RE GOING TO DO
NOW AND DO IT.

William Durant

ALWAYS BE
YOURSELF.

Life is either a daring adventure or nothing.

Helen Keller

NEVER GIVE UP, FOR
THAT IS JUST THE PLACE
AND TIME THAT THE TIDE
WILL TURN.

Harriet Beecher Stowe

LIFE ISN'T A MATTER
OF MILESTONES, BUT
OF MOMENTS.

Rose Kennedy

A negative mind will never give you a positive life.

Anonymous

SAY YES
TO NEW
ADVENTURES.

BEGIN WHATEVER
YOU HAVE TO DO:
THE BEGINNING OF A
WORK STANDS FOR
THE WHOLE.

Ausonius

THE TRICK IS TO ENJOY LIFE.
DON'T WISH AWAY YOUR
DAYS, WAITING FOR BETTER
ONES AHEAD.

Marjorie Pay Hinckley

OPPORTUNITIES MULTIPLY
AS THEY ARE SEIZED.

Sun Tzu

Life is to be enjoyed, not just endured.

Gordon B. Hinckley

If it doesn't challenge you, it doesn't change you.

TRY TO BE A RAINBOW IN SOMEONE'S CLOUD.

Maya Angelou

The best dreams happen when you're awake.

Cherie Gilderbloom

LIFE IS WAY TOO SHORT TO
SPEND ANOTHER DAY AT
WAR WITH **YOURSELF.**

Ritu Ghatourey

IN THE MIDDLE OF
DIFFICULTY LIES
OPPORTUNITY.

Albert Einstein

THE SUN
IS ALWAYS
SHINING
SOMEWHERE
IN THE
WORLD.

IN THE DEPTHS OF WINTER
I FINALLY LEARNED THAT
THERE WAS IN ME AN
INVINCIBLE SUMMER.

Albert Camus

In order to succeed, we must first believe that we can.

Nikos Kazantzakis

THE PERSON WHO
CAN BRING THE
SPIRIT OF LAUGHTER
INTO A ROOM IS
INDEED BLESSED.

Bennett Cerf

Be the person that people want to talk to.

Trust in dreams, for in them is hidden the gate to eternity.

Khalil Gibran

TALKING IS ALWAYS
POSITIVE. THAT'S WHY I
TALK **TOO MUCH.**

Louis C. K.

LET POSITIVITY HELP YOU AND OTHERS.

IF YOUR SHIP
DOESN'T COME IN,
SWIM OUT TO IT.

Jonathan Winters

TALK TO SOMEONE NEW. YOU COULD MAKE THEIR DAY - AND THEY COULD MAKE YOURS.

**Try to be like the turtle –
at ease in your own shell.**

Bill Copeland

EVERY SAINT HAS A
PAST, AND EVERY SINNER
HAS **A FUTURE.**

Oscar Wilde

YOU CAN HAVE
ANYTHING YOU
WANT IF YOU ARE
WILLING TO GIVE UP
THE BELIEF THAT YOU
CAN'T HAVE IT.

Robert Anthony

The quality, not the longevity, of one's life is what is important.

Martin Luther King Jr

Unexpected twists can add spice to life.

DON'T PUT THE KEY TO HAPPINESS IN SOMEONE ELSE'S POCKET.

Anonymous

I JUST BELIEVE IN THE
GOODWILL OF PEOPLE,
THE POWER OF PEOPLE TO
DO SOMETHING POSITIVE.

Eddie Izzard

You create your opportunities by asking for them.

Shakti Gawain

YOU CAN DO IT.
ALL YOU HAVE
TO DO IS TRY.

ALWAYS LAUGH
WHEN YOU CAN. IT IS
CHEAP MEDICINE.

Lord Byron

WE ARE ALL OF
US STARS, AND
WE DESERVE TO
TWINKLE.

Marilyn Monroe

IF NOT NOW, WHEN? IF NOT YOU, WHO?

Good words are worth much, and cost little.

George Herbert

FREEDOM LIES IN BEING BOLD.

Robert Frost

STILL ROUND THE CORNER
THERE MAY WAIT, A NEW
ROAD OR A SECRET GATE.

J. R. R. Tolkien

Always be yourself, express yourself, have faith in yourself, do not go out and look for a successful personality and duplicate it.

Bruce Lee

Each day is a blank canvas... make some marks.

SEVEN DAYS
WITHOUT LAUGHTER
MAKES **ONE WEAK.**

Mort Walker

HOPE WILL NEVER
BE SILENT.

Harvey Milk

With confidence, you
have won even before
you have started.

Marcus Garvey

WELCOME THE DAY'S CHALLENGES.

PESSIMISM LEADS
TO WEAKNESS,
OPTIMISM TO
POWER.

William James

LOVE ALL, TRUST A FEW, DO WRONG TO NONE.

William Shakespeare

NEW CONNECTIONS LEAD TO NEW POSSIBILITIES.

The limits of the possible can only be defined by going beyond them into the impossible.

Arthur C. Clarke

THE GOOD LIFE IS ONE
INSPIRED BY LOVE AND
GUIDED BY **KNOWLEDGE.**

Bertrand Russell

WHEREVER YOU
GO, GO WITH ALL
YOUR HEART.

Confucius

**Delete the negative;
accentuate the positive!**

Donna Karan

YOU ONLY GET ONE
CHANCE AT LIFE AND YOU
HAVE TO GRAB IT **BOLDLY.**

Bear Grylls

Your life is a piece of art – it deserves to be enjoyed.

WE BUILD TOO MANY
WALLS AND NOT
ENOUGH BRIDGES.

Isaac Newton

EVERY MOMENT IS A
FRESH BEGINNING.

T. S. Eliot

A rolling stone gathers no moss.

Proverb

ENJOYMENT IS JUST
THE SOUND OF
BEING CENTRED.

Bhagwan Shree Rajneesh

Be
original.

If you're interested in finding out more about our books, find us on Facebook at **Summersdale Publishers** and follow us on Twitter at **@Summersdale**.

www.summersdale.com